ALPINE SOUTH

PLANTS
AND PLANT COMMUNITES
OF THE HIGH ELEVATIONS
OF THE SOUTHERN APPALACHIANS

L. L. GADDY

ISBN 978-0-615-90598-3
Library of Congress Control Number: 2013954321

terra incognita books

www.tibooks.org

Images by L. L. Gaddy unless otherwise noted.

Cover: Pennsylvania sedge (*Carex pensylvanica*) glade under beech, yellow birch, and buckeye, in beech gap, Mount Hardy Gap, North Carolina.
Dedication (facing page): pink shell azalea (*Rhododendron vaseyi*).
Title Page: Smoky Mountains from Waterrock Knob.
Pages 14-15: Roan Mountain Sunrise, Roan High Knob taken from Round Bald, by Scott Hotaling.

DEDICATION

Sherrie Lynn Ford
(1946-2011)

Harriet Rankin White
(1948-2012)

TABLE OF CONTENTS

Summer thunderstorm in the southeast seen from Round Bald on the Roan Mountain Massif.

INTRODUCTION

"Alpine" South? No, there are no classic alpine elevations in the southeastern United States. But it is all relative. One can get into a car (or on a motorcycle) on a steamy summer day in Charlotte, Birmingham, Richmond, Atlanta, or Columbia, when the thermometer hovers around 100 degrees and the humidity approaches 100 percent, and drive for a few hours into the southern Appalachian Mountains and find an alpine experience. The climate and the vegetation of the highest elevations of our southern mountains are not unlike that of the Adirondacks, New England, or even Canada. Lowlanders of the Southeast have flocked to the Smokies, the Black Mountains, the Roan Mountain area, Mount Rogers, and the Monongahelas for over a century to get away from tropical heat and humidity. Summer colonies in the Linville and the Highlands areas in North Carolina have existed since the early 1800s. In the heat of the Columbia summer, the governor of South Carolina would take a train to West Union (near Walhalla) where the railroad ended, get in a horse-drawn coach, and ascend the Blue Ridge Front to High Hampton (near Cashiers) to escape the heat. It was a two day trip.

Nowadays, with the advent of the Interstate Highway System, one can get to the high mountains of the southern Appalachians from about anywhere in Southeast in less than a day. Furthermore, the establishment of the Great Smoky Mountain National Park in the 1930s and the construction of the Blue Ridge Parkway have made many formerly inaccessible areas of the southern Appalachians easy to reach. The Smokies and the Blue Ridge Parkway are today the most visited units of the National Park Service, both with more visitors than the most popular western national parks (i.e., Yellowstone and Yosemite). The Parkway allows quick and relatively easy access to the Smokies (from the east), the Balsams, Mount Pisgah, the Craggies, the Black Mountains, Linville Gorge, and Grandfather Mountain. One can drive to the rocky slopes of the Craggies in three hours from central South Carolina and find rare high elevation plants that are common in Canada.

The high mountains of the southern Appalachians have fascinated travelers since Hernando de Soto and Juan Pardo explored the Appalachians in the 1500s. Later famous visitors to the region included the naturalist/explorer William Bartram and the French botanist Andre Michaux in the 1700s and Harvard botanist Asa Gray and North Carolina scientist Elisha Mitchell in the 1800s. William Brewster, a Harvard ornithologist who visited the region in the late 1800s, was one of the first scientists to comment on the biogeography of the high elevations of the southern Appalachians. In an 1886 paper on the region, while describing the life zones of the Black Mountains, he wrote of the "Carolinian" Zone of the low elevations, the "Alleghanian" Zone of the mid-elevations, and the "Canadian" Zone of the highest elevations.

The life zones of the highest elevations of the southern Appalachians are indeed similar to those of Canada and New England. Temperatures on Mount Mitchell rarely range above 80° F in summer and frequently fall below zero in winter. Snow is heavy above 4000 feet, and, like areas far to the North, the growing season is short. Because of high rainfall and snowfall and abundant fog precipitation, some have used the term "temperate rainforest" to describe the vegetation of the high southern Appalachians, comparing the region to the mountains of the Pacific Northwest.

In the high elevations of the southern Appalachians, we find isolated islands of plants and plant communities reminiscent of a flora and vegetation normally found considerably north of the region. The spruce-fir communities of our high mountains give one the illusion of being in New England or southern Canada. The Fraser fir (*Abies fraseri*) of the southern Appalachians is only slightly different from the balsam fir (*Abies balsamae*) of Canada, an important constituent of the boreal forest. (Balsam fir actually has several disjunct populations in northern Virginia and West Virginia.) The red spruce (*Picea rubens*) of our high mountains ranges up the Appalachians into the Adirondacks, New England, and on north to Quebec and Nova Scotia in Canada. The yellow birch (*Betula alleghaniensis*) and sugar maple (*Acer saccharum*) of our southern highland "Northern Hardwoods" plant community are also common in the Adirondacks, New England, and southern Canada, and the "Northern Red Oak" or gray oak (*Quercus rubra* var. *ambigua*) forests at around 5000 feet in North Carolina, Tennessee, and Virginia are reminiscent of oak communities far north of the southeastern United States.

Numerous northern plant species range south to the highest elevations of the southern Appalachians. Green alder (*Alnus viridis* ssp. *crispus*), which is known from Alaska and Greenland, reaches the southern limits of its range on the Roan Mountain Massif. Wineleaf cinquefoil [*Sibbaldiopsis (Potentilla) tridentata*)], known from high elevation rocky peaks south to southern North Carolina and northern Georgia, is common in New England and Canada and is found as far north as Greenland. Heart-leaved paperbirch (*Betula cordifolia*), found on the slopes of Mount Mitchell, is known from Newfoundland and Quebec; New England ragwort [*Packera (Senecio) schweinitizana*], common on high southern Appalachian balds, ranges to Nova Scotia and Quebec; and the large purple-fringed orchid (*Platanthera grandiflora*), found in openings in spruce-fir in North Carolina, grows in Newfoundland and Ontario.

The high elevations of the southern Appalachians are also noteworthy for unique and endemic plants. Fraser fir (*Abies fraseri*), the dominant tree on the highest southern Appalachian mountains, is found only in Virginia, North Carolina, and Tennessee as is Gray's lily (*Lilium grayi*). Bent avens (*Geum geniculatum*), spreading avens (*Geum radiatum*), the Blue Ridge goldenrod (*Solidago spithamea*), and Rugel's ragwort (*Rugelia nudicaulis*) are known only from Tennessee and North Carolina. The beautiful pink-shell azalea (*Rhododendron vaseyi*) is found in North Carolina and on Rabun Bald in northwest Georgia. The deep-blue Balsam Mountain gentian (*Gentiana latidens*) is found only in North Carolina.

This book is a brief guide to the plants and plant communities of our "Alpine" South—the high elevations of the southern Appalachians. It covers the montane regions of Georgia, North Carolina, Tennessee, Virginia, and West Virginia from elevations of 4000 feet up to the highest peaks in each state. Mount Mitchell and the Black Mountains, Clingman's Dome and the Smokies, Waterrock Knob and the Plott Balsam Mountains, Richland Balsam and the Great Balsam Mountains, Craggy Dome of the Great Craggy Mountains, and the highest peaks of the Roan Mountain Massif in North Carolina and Tennessee are all over 6000 feet elevation. In Virginia, Mount Rogers, Whitetop Mountain, and Haw Orchard Mountain are the only summits over 5000 feet, but there are nearly 100 other peaks over 4000 feet. In West Virginia, Spruce Knob is the highest point at 4863 feet, but there are more than 150 peaks above 4000 feet.

Four thousand feet is somewhat arbitrary, but at that elevation or just a few hundred feet below, one begins to see elements of the flora of the more northern Appalachians. I have included a few sites just below 4000 feet—the Cranberry Glades, Dolly Sods (both in WVA), Linville Gorge, and Looking Glass Rock (the latter two in NC)—because they are sites that harbor noteworthy "alpine" and northern species and/or plant communities.

The images that follow were captured by me (unless otherwise noted) from 1979, when I first began to notice that one could really find the vegetation, the flora, and the feel of the far North in the southern Appalachians, to the present. As may be seen below, many of these images are from my favorite high elevation locales—places that I have visited and revisited and enjoyed over the last few decades. I hope you enjoy this journey as much as I have.

Old-growth yellow birch in northern hardwoods on the southern Blue Ridge Parkway, Wagon Road Gap.

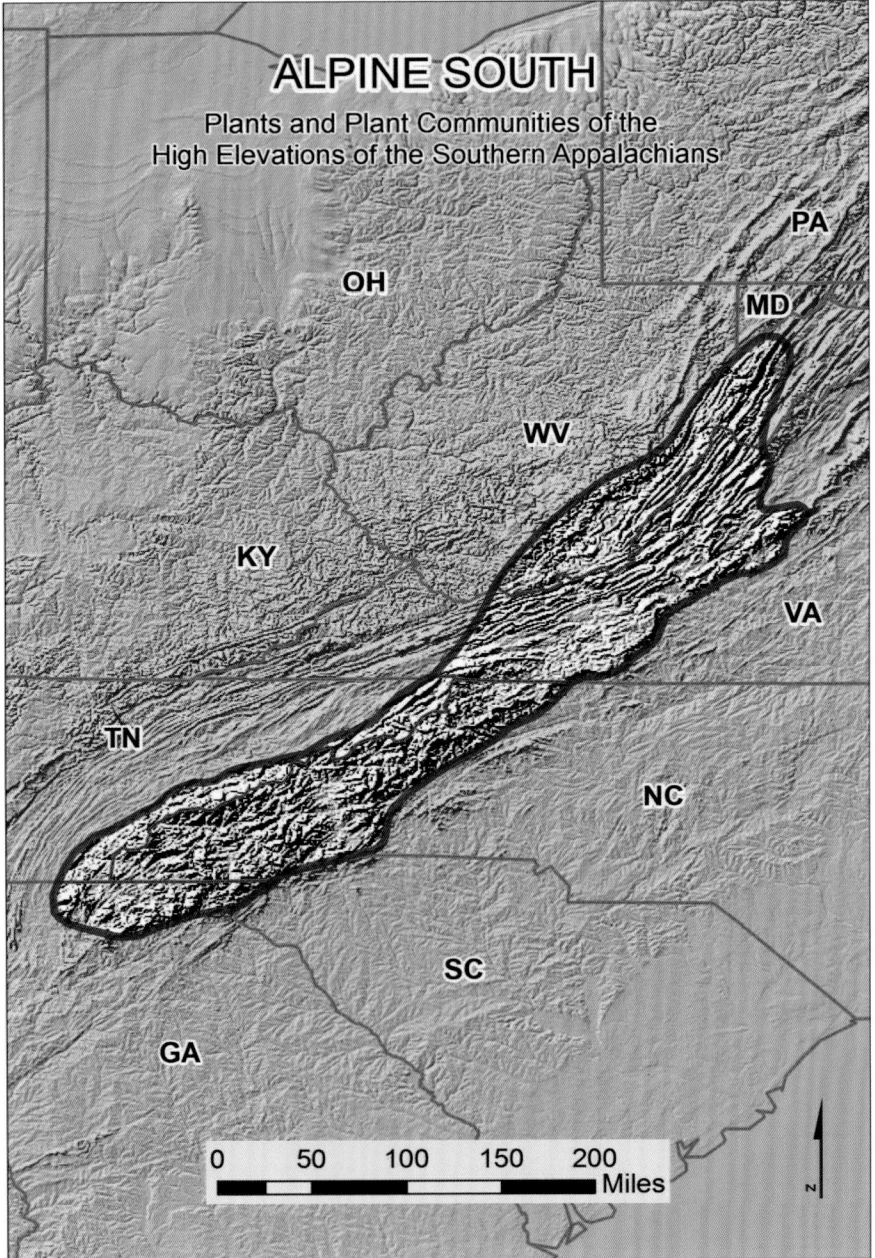

ALPINE SOUTH
Plants and Plant Communities of the
High Elevations of the Southern Appalachians

PA

OH

MD

WV

KY

VA

TN

NC

SC

GA

0	50	100	150	200
Miles

N

The lower Smoky Mountains from the spruce-fir zone on the road to Clingman's Dome.

The sun sets on the southern Appalachians on a summer day; view from Round Bald, Roan Mt.

Rainbow over the Blue Ridge Parkway from Craggy Pinnacle.

Foggy summer day in the spruce-fir of the Black Mts. looking north from Mt. Mitchell.

Grandfather Mountain seen from the west.

MOUNTAIN RANGES, GEOLOGY, AND CLIMATE

MOUNTAIN RANGES

The highest mountains of the high elevations of the southern Appalachians are in North Carolina and Tennessee. There are six ranges therein with peaks over 6000 feet—the Black Mountains, the Great Balsams, the Great Craggy Mountains, the Great Smoky Mountains, the Plott Balsams, and the Roan Mountain Massif (Table 1). The Smokies have the greatest number of peaks above 6000 feet, with the Blacks and the Great Balsams close behind. There are over 40 peaks in North Carolina and Tennessee over 6000 feet in elevation. In Virginia, there are three peaks above 5000 feet and over 100 above 4000 feet. West Virginia has over 150 peaks above 4000 feet in elevation, none over 5000 feet.

Table 1. Major mountain ranges and highest peaks in the southern Appalachians.

Mountain Range	Highest Peak	States
Allegheny Mountains[1]	Spruce Knob 4863'	WV
Bald Mountains	Big Bald 5516'	NC-TN
Black Mountains	Mount Mitchell 6684'	NC
Blue Ridge	Grandfather Mountain 5946'	WV-VA-NC-SC-GA
Cheoah Mountains	Cheoah Bald 5062'	NC
Cowee Mountains	Yellow Mountain 5125'	NC
Great Balsam Mountains	Richland Balsam 6410'	NC
Great Craggy Mountains	Craggy Dome ca. 6100'	NC
Great Smoky Mountains	Clingman's Dome 6643'	NC-TN
Mount Rogers Massif	Mount Rogers 5729'	VA
Nantahala Mountains	Standing Indian 5499'	NC
Newfound Mountains	Sandy Mush Bald 5152'	NC
Pisgah Ridge	Mount Pisgah 5721'	NC
Plott Balsam Mountains	Waterrock Knob 6292'	NC
Roan Mountain Massif[2]	Roan High Knob 6285'	NC-TN
Snowbird Mountains	Teyahalee Bald 4716'	NC
Tusquitee Mountains	Tusquitee Bald 5240'	NC
Unaka Mountains	Unaka Mountain ca. 5200'	TN
Unicoi Mountains	Huckleberry Knob 5560'	NC-TN

[1]Some writers exclude the Allegheny Mountains, which extend into Maryland and Pennsylvania, from the southern Appalachians. Here, they are included in the high elevations of the southern Appalachians due to the number of 4000'+ peaks that are known from the West Virginia Alleghenies.

[2]The Roan Mountain Massif/Complex of mountains is often included in the Unaka Mountain Range to the southwest in Tennessee. Here, the Roan Mountain Massif is considered separate from the Unakas.

GEOLOGY

From a distance, the Appalachians from the Alleghenies of West Virginia down to the Smokies appear similar in origin and structure. A closer look, however, reveals a diverse assemblage of mountains, rocks, and rock formations created by continental collision, thrusting, faulting, folding, intrusion, and subsequent erosion over millions of years. The oldest rocks to have been dated from the southern Appalachians, collected from the Roan Mountain Massif, are approximately 1.8 billion years old. Geologists, therefore, think that our highlands were originally formed during the uplift of the Grenville orogeny in the Proterozoic Era approximately two billion years ago. Later, during the Alleghanian orogeny, a collision by the North American tectonic plate with the supercontinent Gondwanaland pushed up the proto-Appalachian mountain range. Thrust sheets from offshore volcanic arcs slid over the existing continental crust, and subsequent uplift and erosion produced (in the southern Appalachians) the Blue Ridge, as we now know it, and its accompanying back "ranges" and geological formations. These include the Blacks, the Smokies, the Craggies, the Great Balsams, the Plott Balsams, the Roan Massif, and smaller ranges. Differential erosion exposed basement rocks (under the thrust sheets) such as the Grandfather Mountain "window," the Blowing Rock gneiss, and the Chilhowee quartzite in and around Linville Gorge.

In contrast to the granitic and metamorphic rocks of the Blue Ridge, a diversity of rock types and formations may be seen in some of the back ranges, windows, and fault zones. Older metamorphic rocks such as metagraywacke boulders can be seen in the Grandfather Mountain window under the Linn Cove viaduct of the Blue Ridge Parkway, and the resistant metamorphic rock of the Black Mountains, the highest North American mountain range east of the Black Hills of South Dakota, are found parallel to and west of the Blue Ridge Escarpment.

Farther to the west of the Blue Ridge is the Great Smoky Mountains. Here, a complex of rock formations composed of schist, sandstones, siltstones, and slate have been folded and faulted (there are four major faults in the Smokies) and pushed up over up over younger rocks (the limestone of Cades Cove is a "window" of younger rock). On the roadcut on the way to Newfound Gap, one can see the Anakeesta Formation, a complex of meta-siltstones, rust-colored from the oxidation of pyrite (fool's gold). This same formation underlies Charlie's Bunion and "The Sawteeth" on the Appalachian Trail, east of Mt. Kephart.

Elsewhere in the southern Appalachian high elevations, eroded intrusions such as Looking Glass Rock (igneous quartz diorite) and the igneous plutonic domes of the Highlands-Cashiers area are interspersed within the Blue Ridge. And to the north, Mount Rogers and Whitetop Mountain, the tallest mountains in Virginia, are domes of rhyolite, an igneous volcanic rock. Farther north, the Allegheny Mountains in West Virginia are thought to be a back formation of folded sedimentary (sandstone) and metamorphic (quartzite) rocks, reaching almost 5000 feet at Spruce Knob on the West Virginia-Virginia border.

CLIMATE

The climate of the high elevations of the southern Appalachians is very unlike that of most of the southeastern United States. There is more precipitation, summers are cooler, and winters are colder. Table 2 compares the mean temperatures and precipitation of several high mountain locations with other well-known sites. The mean high temperature in July in Columbia, South Carolina is 92.7°F, while on the highest peaks (Mt. Mitchell, Clingman's Dome, and Mt. LeConte) of the southern Appalachians in North Carolina and Tennessee, the mean July maximum is around 65° F. The annual rainfall is 10-40 inches more in the higher elevations than in the southeastern lowlands. And the yearly snowfall, of course, is not even comparable to southern lowland sites. Mt. Mitchell gets almost as much snow (over 92 inches) per year as Lake Placid, New York in the Adirondacks, and Grandfather Mt. and Mt. LeConte get about the same amount of snow as Bangor, Maine.

The blue of the Blue Ridge and the smoke of the Smoky Mountains are apparitions created by fog and low, misty clouds. There is evidence that almost 50 percent of the precipitation in the Smokies is fog and mist. The southern Appalachians have nearly as many fog days as do the Pacific Northwest and the Canadian Maritimes, two famously foggy regions. (The high elevation climate of the southern Appalachians has, in fact, been called a "marine west coast" or "temperate rainforest' climate.) And if you are lucky and happen to be in the high mountains when fog and mist freeze on to the trees, you will get to see one of the most beautiful of weather phenomena—rime ice.

Table 2. Climatic data from southern Appalachian and other stations.[1]

Station	Elevation (approx.)	State	July[2] Mean Max	January Mean Min	Annual Rainfall	Annual Snowfall
Asheville	2100'	NC	84.0	26.7	45.6	9.9
Bangor	160'	ME	79.4	6.7	41.9	66.1
Beech Mt.	**5000'**	**NC**	**68.9**	**19.1**	**51.5**	--
Blowing Rock	3600'	NC	76.7	20.4	63.7	--
Boone	3200'	NC	78.9	20.7	52.7	35.7
Burlington	330'	VT	80.9	10.2	36.8	81.2
Celo	2600'	NC	78.9	24.2	57.9	6.1
Charlotte	740'	NC	89.0	29.6	41.6	4.3
Clingman's Dome	**6600"**	**NC**	**65.0**	**19.0**	**82.1**	--
Columbia	300'	SC	92.7	33.7	44.6	1.5
Gatlinburg	1450'	TN	86.6	25.2	55.3	8.9
Grandfather Mt.	**5800'**	**NC**	**70.5**	**19.9**	**53.5**	**61.2**
Highlands	**4100'**	**NC**	**79.5**	**24.2**	**84.5**	**11.8**
Knoxville	800'	TN	88.2	29.2	47.9	6.5
Lake Placid	1800'	NY	77.1	5.4	41.0	108.0
Mt. LeConte	**6600'**	**TN**	**65.9**	**17.3**	**73.5**	**71.8**
Mt. Mitchell	**6600'**	**NC**	**65.9**	**17.0**	**74.2**	**92.3**

[1]Data based on years 1981-2010 (from National Climatic Data Center, Asheville, NC, www.noaa.gov).
[2]Temperature in degrees Fahrenheit; --Data not available; **Bold indicates high elevation stations in southern Appalachians.**

Fog precipitation is a significant portion of the annual moisture in the high elevations.

Winter wonderland on the southern Blue Ridge Parkway at 5000 feet.

Two-inch deep hail after summer thunderstorm at 5200 feet on Blue Ridge Parkway.

White-out on north slopes of Mount LeConte, Great Smoky Mountains.

PLANT COMMUNITES

SPRUCE-FIR

The highest mountains of the southern Appalachians are vegetated with forests of fir and spruce in which the canopy is dominated by Fraser fir (*Abies fraseri*), red spruce (*Picea rubens*), or a combination of these two needle-leaved evergreen species. Most of the major southern Appalachian peaks above 5000 feet and all of the peaks above 6000 feet are vegetated with elements of this community type. Fraser fir is naturally found at elevations of 5000 feet or above; red spruce ranges down to 2500 feet in the Smokies, but it most common at 4500 to 6000 feet. Fraser fir is closely related to the more northern balsam fir (*Abies balsamae*) and is often referred to as the balsam fir—hence, the names Balsam Mountain, Black Balsam, the Plott Balsams, the Great Balsam Mountains, all fir-covered mountains. Early settlers to the southern Appalachians thought the Fraser fir was the female and the red spruce was the male of the same species. The terminology "she"-balsam (Fraser fir) and "he"-balsam (red spruce), therefore, was born and has persisted to this day in the vernacular of mountain people.

Balsam woolly adelgid (aphid) (*Adelges piceae*) is a small insect that, contrary to its scientific name, attacks fir, not spruce. It was introduced into the United States around 1900 from Europe and was discovered in southern Appalachian populations of Fraser fir in the 1950s. Since then, it has decimated Fraser fir populations in the region. Ghost forests of dead firs are still conspicuous in the Blacks and the Smokies. It is estimated that 95 percent of the fir the Smokies was killed by the adelgid. Seedlings and saplings are generally immune to the insect; one, therefore, often finds healthy young fir forests amid the ghost forests. Although the insect does not attack spruce, the death of most mature firs has changed the nature of the forest, causing tree fall and wind damage to the remaining spruce in spruce-fir stands. Some researchers have noted that acid precipitation and logging history have exacerbated the impact of the balsam woolly adelgid in the high elevation forests of the southern Appalachians, preventing complete recovery of the forests.

Other trees found in the canopy and sub-canopy of the Spruce-Fir Forest include heart-leaved birch (*Betula cordifolia*) (in the Black Mountains), yellow birch (*Betula alleghaniensis*), mountain maple (*Acer spicatum*), and mountain ash (*Sorbus americana*). The spruce-fir lower strata is dominated by the ever-present hobblebush (*Viburnum lantanoides*), but often has dense thickets of Catawba rhododendron (*Rhododendron catawbiense*) [or Carolina rhododendron (*R. carolinianum*)] and, in openings, glades of mountain woodfern (*Dryopteris campyloptera*). The ground layer of the spruce-fir forest is nothing like that of any other southern Appalachian forest. In the dark shade of the evergreens, thick mats of moss (most commonly *Hylocomium splendens*) often cover the forest floor interspersed with young Fraser fir and the striking flowers of the wood sorrel (*Oxalis montana*). In openings where Fraser fir has died off and not regenerated, thickets of Allegheny (*Rubus allegheniensis*) and smooth (*R. canadensis*) blackberry may be interspersed with herbaceous species such as the rare large purple-fringed orchid (*Platanthera grandiflora*).

The soft balsam-scented needles of Fraser fir on left; the prickly red spruce needles on right.

Flag-form (wind sculpted) Fraser fir on Grandfather Mountain.

Young Fraser fir invading disease-damaged area on Clingman's Dome.

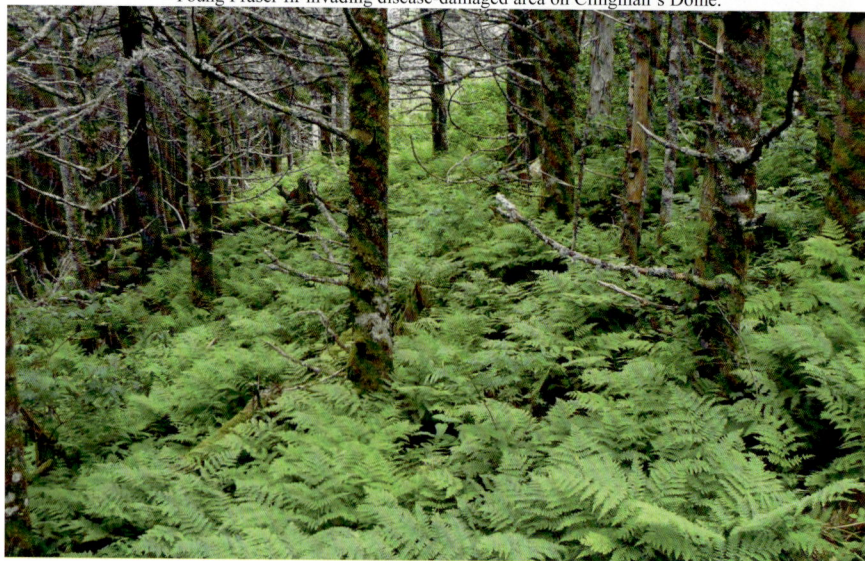
Mountain woodfern carpets the understory of a Fraser fir forest on Mount Mitchell.

Dwarfed, spreading red spruce on Spruce Knob (4863 feet) in West Virginia.

Pure stand of mature, dwarfed red spruce on Whitetop Mountain in Virginia.

NORTHERN HARDWOOD FORESTS

The Northern Hardwood Forest is widespread at high elevations in the southern Appalachians. The typical northern hardwood forest is dominated by yellow birch (*Betula alleghaniensis*), American beech (*Fagus grandifolia*), and yellow buckeye (*Aesculus flava*) (red spruce is often mixed with this type at higher elevations). A richer-site type may also have sugar maple (*Acer saccharum*) in the canopy with white ash (*Fraxinus americana*) and basswood (*Tilia heterophylla*) (in addition to yellow birch, beech, and buckeye) and an understory of rich herbs such as doll's eye (*Actaea pachypoda*) and blue cohosh (*Caulophyllum thalictroides*). The High Elevation Boulderfield has enormous boulders (to over 25 feet in height) scattered among a forest of yellow birch and American beech. Finally, the Beech Gap type of northern hardwood forest is pure, dwarfed American beech usually with glades of Pennsylvania sedge (*Carex pensylvanica*) in the understory. Beech gaps are usually found in high elevation gaps from 4500 to 6000 feet in elevation. Here, what is often referred to as "red" or "gray" beech may form low, clonal thickets only slightly taller than shrub level.

The Rich-Site Northern Hardwoods is common, among other places, on the north slopes of Sugar Mountain near Banner Elk and on high elevation slopes north of Boone. The High Elevation Boulderfield is common on the western slopes of Sugar Mountain, on the eastern slopes of Grandfather Mountain (under and below Linn Cove Viaduct on the Parkway), and at Steestachee and Wesner Boulderfields near MP 438 on the Blue Ridge Parkway. Some rich high elevation sites appear to be mixtures of rich-site Northern Hardwood, the High Elevation Boulderfield, and the High Elevation Cove types.

Finally, the Beech Gap type is scattered in gaps in the Smokies, but is more accessible along the Parkway at Bullhead Gap (ca. MP 360) and Mount Hardy Gap (ca. MP 426) (see cover of book for image). The beech gap at Mount Hardy Gap also has yellow birch and yellow buckeye and a rich understory with Pennsylvania sedge, erect trillium (*Trillium erectum*) and Carolina spring beauty (*Claytonia caroliniana*).

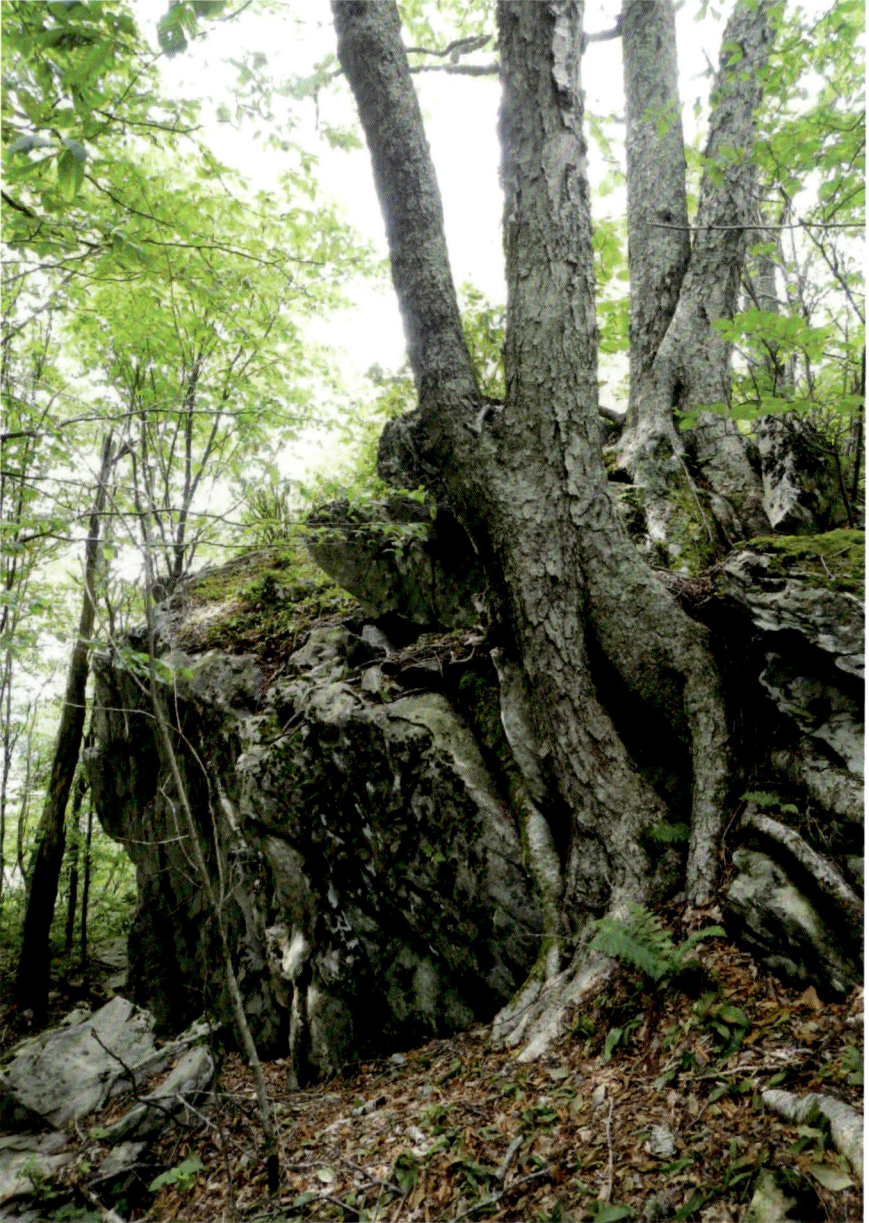

Yellow birch growing on and around boulders in a High Elevation Boulderfield Forest at 4800 feet on Sugar Mountain near Banner Elk, NC.

Mature yellow birch, beech, sugar maple, and white basswood in rich Northern Hardwood Forest near Banner Elk, NC.

Understory of Beech Gap Forest in Bullhead Gap (elevation 5600 feet) just north of Craggy Dome ("grassy" understory is dominated by Pennsylvania sedge).

Pennsylvania sedge in Beech Gap Forest, Mt. Hardy Gap, NC.

Northern hardwood forest interspersed with red spruce and sarvisberry, southern Blue Ridge Parkway.

Beech Gap Forest below grassy bald on Big Bald (TN-NC border).

HIGH ELEVATION OAK FORESTS

Oak forests are common and widespread at high elevations in the southern Appalachians. Their composition, however, is very different from that of lower elevation oak forests. First of all, only a few species of oaks are commonly found above 4000 feet—gray oak (*Quercus rubra var. ambigua*), red oak (*Quercus rubra*), white oak (*Quercus alba*), chestnut oak (*Quercus montana*), scarlet oak (*Quercus coccinea*), and black oak (*Quercus velutina*), the latter three of which are somewhat rare above this elevation.

High Elevation Oak Forests that occur on or near rock outcrops, on ridges, or in high elevation gaps tend to be dwarfed forests or forests with a low canopy. On Frying Pan Ridge on the southern Blue Ridge Parkway, an excellent, nearly pure, gray oak forest with a canopy of 50-60 feet is present. In high elevation gaps and along the margins of grassy and heath balds, a dwarfed, open oak forest called the "oak orchard" forest may be present. Here, open, stunted trees are interspersed amongst a rich understory of high elevation grasses, sedges, and herbs. A good example of this type can be seen east of Big Bald in the Bald Mountains. The "montane white oak" forest is another dwarfed oak forest of high elevations. Small, mature (over 200 years old at some sites), white oak from 50 feet to only 10 feet tall dominates, often with heath species and other species of dwarfed oaks. On Rabun Bald and Scaly Mountain, scarlet oak often dominates or complements the dwarfed white oak forest. It, along with black oak, can also be seen on other high elevation peaks northwest of Highlands, NC. Other examples of the Montane White Oak community subtype are on Laurel Knob, in Jackson County, North Carolina, and on Bluff Mountain, in Ashe County, North Carolina.

Finally, red oak-dominated forests are sometimes found in the upper reaches of high elevation coves. Here, mature red oak blends with white ash (*Fraxinus americana*), basswood (*Tilia heterophylla*), and sugar maple (*Acer saccharum*). The understory of this type is rich in herbaceous species. A Red Oak Rich Cove subtype is found on Sugar Mountain near Banner Elk, North Carolina and in rich, amphibolite coves north of Boone.

Old-growth northern red oak in flower in early May on Frying Pan Ridge, Blue Ridge Parkway.

Mature northern red or "gray" oak in high elevation forest in North Carolina.

Dwarfed white oak in high elevation "montane" white oak community on Bluff Mt., Ashe Co., NC.

HIGH ELEVATION COVE FORESTS

For the wildflower lover, there is no better place to be in spring than walking in an Appalachian cove forest. The Rich Cove Forest type is among the southern Appalachian plant communities with the greatest species richness, especially in the herbaceous layer. Some high elevation cove forests rival their lower elevation counterparts in floristic diversity. In the High Elevation Cove Forest type, the canopy dominants are usually yellow buckeye (*Aesculus flava*), basswood (*Tilia heterophylla*), sugar maple (*Acer saccharum*), white ash (*Fraxinus americana*), and, occasionally, Canada hemlock (*Tsuga canadensis*) [tulip poplar (*Liriodendron tulipifera*) is usually not present above 4000 feet]. The composition of the herbaceous layer in the High Elevation Cove Forest varies from cove to cove based on shrub layer, exposure, and soil type. This type is sometimes difficult to distinguish from the Northern Hardwood Boulderfield and the rich-site Northern Hardwood type; all three of these types are often found just above the elevation limits of tulip poplar (3800-4000 feet) where the Rich Cove Forest type grades into higher elevation types.

Rich coves along the southern Blue Ridge Parkway above Waynesville (NC) have trillium glades mixed with the brilliant blue of dwarf larkspur (*Delphinium tricorne*) (usually found below 4000 feet). In the Craggies, Virginia spiderwort (*Tradescantia virginiana*), eastern columbine (*Aquilegia canadensis*), and large-leaved waterleaf (*Hydrophyllum macrophyllum*) can be found in rich, high elevation coves. North of Asheville, high elevation coves have more large-flowered trillium (*Trillium grandiflorum*) than do the more southern coves, which usually have more erect trillium (*Trillium erectum*). And around Boone, the amphibolite-rich coves have another unique mixture of interesting cove species.

Good high elevation coves can be found in the Great Balsam Mountains above Waynesville (NC) on the slopes of the Blue Ridge Parkway (around MP 438, downslope from the Steestachee and Wesner Boulderfields) and in the north-facing cove below Licklog Gap (MP 436-7); in the Craggies (near MP 373 on the Parkway); on the northwest slopes of Roan Mountain at 4000-5200 feet in Tennessee; Banks Creek Cove west of Burnsville, North Carolina (a spectacular, privately-owned/protected cove ranging to 5200 feet); and below Courthouse Rock (on Sugarlands Mountain southwest of U. S. 441) and above Porter's Flat (upstream from Greenbrier Cove), the latter two sites in Great Smoky Mountain National Park.

Yellowstone Falls, on the upper Pigeon River, drops into a High Elevation Cove forest.

Same view, early spring.   Graveyard Fields, southern Blue Ridge Parkway.

Larkspur at 4400 feet: High Elevation Cove Forest, near Waynesville, NC.

High Elevation Cove forest at ca. 4500 feet in NC with basswood, buckeye, yellow birch, and dead hemlock.

Trillium cove along southern Blue Ridge Parkway near Waynesville, NC.

Large-leaved waterleaf in High Elevation Cove Forest in the southern Craggies (NC).

Large-flowered bellwort in cove at 4600 feet in NC.

Large clump of erect trillium at 4800 feet just south of Asheville, NC.

HEMLOCK FORESTS

Two species of hemlock are known from the high elevations of the southern Appalachians: Canada hemlock, eastern hemlock, or spruce-pine (*Tsuga canadensis*) and Carolina hemlock (*Tsuga caroliniana*). The Canada Hemlock Forest type is generally a community of lower elevation acidic forests and coves. Pure stands of Canada hemlock are absent from the high elevations, but scattered trees of this species can be found up to 5000 feet in the southern Appalachians. In the higher elevations, Canada hemlock occurs in the High Elevation Cove type and on mid-elevation (4000 to 5000 feet) ridges and slopes with oaks (primarily *Quercus rubra*) and occasionally mixes in with lower elevation northern hardwoods. Canada hemlocks can be seen up to 5200 feet on the Blue Ridge Parkway. Carolina hemlock, on the other hand, is a tree of rocky bluffs, cliffs, and gorge walls. Most Carolina hemlock bluffs are below 4000 feet, but it is not unusual to find the Carolina Hemlock Bluff community type above that elevation. Carolina hemlocks can be seen at above 5000 feet in the Craggies and on Bluff Mountain in Ashe County, NC.

Both trees have become victims of the hemlock woolly adelgid (*Adelges tsugae*), which was introduced into the United States from eastern Asia in 1924 and made its way to eastern U. S. by the late 1960s. Since then, these insects have been found from Massachusetts to Georgia in stands of both species of hemlock. The adelgid, unlike the balsam woolly adelgid, attacks trees of all ages. Stricken trees show a cottony-white exudation at the base of the needles. Although there are pockets where healthy stands of hemlocks of both species are found (the hemlocks of south-central West Virginia, for example, seem much healthier than those in North Carolina and Tennessee), at the current rate of tree death in the southern Appalachians, the healthy hemlock stand will soon be a memory of the past.

Canada hemlock-dominated forests were once abundant (as dead trees indicate) from 4000 to 5200 feet on Spruce Pine Ridge in the Craggies, and large, dead Canada hemlock trees can be seen in the High Elevation Cove Forest below Yellowstone Falls in the Graveyard Fields area of the Blue Ridge Parkway. Remnant Carolina Hemlock can be seen on Looking Glass Rock, on lower Craggy Dome, and, finally, a good, healthy stand of Carolina hemlock is present on the top of Bluff Mountain (in Ashe County, NC).

Leaves (needles) of Carolina hemlock (left) and Canada or eastern hemlock.

Dead Canada hemlock in High Elevation Cove Forest, headwaters Pigeon River.

Carolina hemlock-montane white oak forest on Bluff Mountain (Ashe County, NC).

Dead hemlock (Canada and Carolina) on the west face of Looking Glass Rock, an NC Granite Dome.

HIGH ELEVATION ROCKY SUMMITS

The High Elevation Rocky Summit plant community type is found on rocky mountain tops over 4000 feet in elevation. Here, on large, open rock outcrops or outcrops amid Fraser fir and red spruce, non-woody species are dominant. Spreading avens (*Geum radiatum*) (a NC-TN endemic), wineleaf cinquefoil (*Sibbaldiopsis tridentata*) (a far-northern peripheral), Michaux's or cliff saxifrage [*Hydatica petiolaris* (=*Saxifraga michauxii*)], mountain oat grass (*Danthonia compressa*), deer-hair bulrush [(*Trichophorum caespitosum ssp. caespitosum* (=*Scirpus caespitosus*)] (a circumboreal peripheral), mountain false-dandelion (*Krigia montana*) (a southern Appalachian endemic), and other non-woody species are found in this type.

Examples of this plant community type are found on Roan High Knob, Roan High Bluff, Grandfather Mountain, Devil's Courthouse (along the southern Parkway), Craggy Pinnacle, and Charlie's Bunion, Mt. LeConte, and Chimney Tops in the Smokies.

Devil's Courthouse, southern Blue Ridge Parkway.

Rocky cliffs with spruce and northern hardwoods on volcanic rhyolite, Whitetop Mountain, Virginia.

The rocky east rim of Linville Gorge (looking south) is approximately 4000 feet in elevation.

Deer-hair bulrush growing in the High Elevation Rocky Summit of Craggy Pinnacle.

HIGH ELEVATION GRANITE DOMES

Granite domes result from the intrusion of igneous rock into a landscape. These intrusions are gradually uplifted and eroded or exfoliated. Erosion of an "exfoliation" dome is similar to the peeling an onion. Sheets of rock gradually break off from freezing and thawing, resulting in a dome-shaped outcrop. Most granite domes have some vegetation on the top and extensive, smooth rock cliffs on the sides. There is historic evidence that the area of exposed rock on some granite domes has expanded in recent times due to fire and subsequent erosion.

Most of the classic High Elevation Granite Domes are in the Highlands-Cashiers area in southern North Carolina. Moving up the Blue Ridge to the north, Looking Glass Rock (just under 4000 feet) is a notable and conspicuous dome that is visible from much of the southern Blue Ridge Parkway. Farther north, Craggy Dome at just over 6000 feet, which has elements of the high elevation granite dome, may be the highest example of this type in the southern Appalachians. Forested and shrub plant communities may be found on granite domes, but the most distinctive community consists of non-woody rock outcrop species.

Twisted spike moss (*Selaginella tortipila*), mountain false-dandelion (*Krigia montana*) (a southern Appalachian endemic), and the granite dome bluet (*Houstonia longifolia var. glabra*) are often seen on high elevation granite domes. Other species seen in this community type include the southern Appalachian endemics Biltmore sedge (*Carex biltmoreana*) (in seepages) and Blue Ridge ragwort [*Packera (Senecio) millefolia*], along with wavy hairgrass [*Avenella (Deschampsia) flexuosa*] and rock harlequin (*Corydalis sempervirens*).

Red spruce (at high elevations), Carolina hemlock (*Tsuga caroliniana*), pitch pine (*Pinus rigida*) (where periodic hot fire has been present), dwarfed red and/or white oak, and eastern red cedar (*Juniperus virginiana*) (at lower elevations) are often seen on granite domes.

Good examples of the High Elevation Granite Dome plant community may be found on Whiteside Mountain, the Fodderstacks, Rock Mountain, Chimneytop Mountain, and Terrapin Mountain, all in the Highlands-Cashiers area in Macon and Jackson Counties, North Carolina.

Whiteside Mountain, a granitic dome near Highlands, NC, is just over 5000 feet in elevation.

Looking Glass Rock, a granitic dome ca. 4000 feet, seen from the Blue Ridge Parkway
(note dead hemlocks near its summit).

Dwarfed pitch pine, eastern red cedar, and spike moss mats on Laurel Knob,
a North Carolina granitic dome near 4500 feet in elevation that overlooks Dillard Canyon near Cashiers, NC.

Craggy Dome (ca. 6000 feet) harbors Rocky Summit, Granite Dome, and Heath Bald communities.

Spike moss mats cover Big Fodderstack, a granite dome near Highlands, NC; the old, dwarfed pitch pine here are up to 400 years old.

The sheer cliffs of Laurel Knob are among the steepest in the southern Appalachians.

HEATH BALDS

Heath balds are so called because of the dominance of shrubs in the heath or azalea family, Ericaceae, therein. The most famous high elevation Heath Bald community in the southern Appalachians is the Catawba rhododendron (*Rhododendron catawbiense*)-dominated heath bald. On non-forested, rocky high-elevation slopes, dense thickets of this shrub have developed at high elevations. In late June and early July when the shrubs flower, spectacular displays of rose, purple, and reddish flowers can be seen. Flower-watching tourists and photographers annually flock to locations such as Roan Mountain, Craggie "Gardens" (in the Great Craggy Mountains), the southern Blue Ridge Parkway, and the Smokies to see these heath balds in flower. Mountain laurel (*Kalmia latifolia*), minnie bush (*Menziesia pilosa*) (an endemic to the central and southern Appalachians), and blueberries (*Vaccinium* spp.) (especially highbush blueberry, *Vaccinium corymbosum*) are often associated with Catawba rhododendron in higher elevation shrub balds.

Heath balds south of Asheville on the southern Blue Ridge Parkway also have mountain fetterbush (*Pieris floribunda*). This spectacular early-flowering shrub has large white, urn-shaped flowers. It is quite common in balds and on road margins in the Devil's Courthouse area (Mileposts 420-430). Carolina rhododendron (*Rhododendron carolinianum*) is more common than Catawba rhododendron in shrubs balds on quartzite, particularly in and around Linville Gorge, and balds on slate and other metamorphic rocks in the Smoky Mountains. Heath balds on Grandfather Mountain and Whiteside Mountain have the low, white-flowering sand myrtle [*Kalmia (Leiophyllum) buxifolia*] mixed with other shrubs as do some heath balds in the Smokies. Satulah Mountain, just south of Whiteside Mountain, has a ground juniper (*Juniperus communis* var. *depressa*)-dominated heath bald.

Catawba rhododendron in shrub bald along margins of grassy bald, Round Mountain, Roan Mt. Massif.

Heath balds are found on the south face of Whiteside Mountain near Highlands, NC.

Mountain laurel in heath bald on the northwest face of Craggy Pinnacle, Blue Ridge Parkway.

GRASSY BALDS

Some of the high peaks of the southern Appalachians have neither forest nor exposed rocks. These grass-covered mountains are generally called grass or grassy "balds." Grassy balds are treeless and shrubless mountaintops dominated by grasses, sedges, and herbs. Because of the question of their origin, more scientific literature probably exists on the subject of grassy balds than any other plant community type in the southern Appalachians. Are grassy balds natural or are they the result of historic human-induced grazing and fire? The answer is complex and may be depend upon which bald is being discussed. Many balds have been cleared and maintained within recent human history (the last 200 years). Some balds have been burned and some balds have been timbered first, then burned. Having grassy mountaintops was a distinct advantage in the days of early settlement of the southern Appalachians. Cattle foraged in cove pastures and often grazed on milksick weed [*Ageratina altissima* var. *roanensis* (*Eupatorium rugosum*)], also called Appalachian white snakeroot. As its name indicates, the milk of the cows that ate milksick weed made humans sick. The early settlers thought that milksickness was caused by cows grazing in cool, shady coves and, therefore, wanted their cows to move up into higher sunny, summer pastures. Having a nearby grassy bald or high elevation pasture was a partial answer to the problem. There is evidence, however, that some grassy balds have been around for centuries. In pre-settlement times, wind storms followed by lightning fires may have cleared these mountaintops, which were later maintained as grassy balds by grazing animals and periodic lightning fires.

One of the most common grasses found in the Grassy Bald plant community type is mountain oat grass (*Danthonia compressa*). It occurs on nearly every grassy bald. Some "grassy" balds are dominated by glades of sedges (*Carex* spp.), which, from a distance, look like grasses. On the Roan Mountain Massif, on Round, Jane, and Grassy Balds, the peripheral green alder (*Alnus viridis* ssp. *crispa*), a shrub, grows in thickets, reaching the southern limits of its range. Indian poke (*Veratrum viride*), Cumberland (*Rhododendron cumberlandense*) and flame (*Rhododendron calendulaceum*) azaleas, New England ragwort [*Packera (Senecio) schweinitziana*], Allegheny (*Rubus allegheniensis*) and smooth (*R. canadensis*) blackberry, Catawba rhododendron, wineleaf cinquefoil (*Sibbaldiopsis tridentata*), and hay-scented ferns (*Dennstaedtia punctilobula*) are among other species commonly seen in the Grassy Bald community type.

Some noteworthy grassy balds are Round Bald on Roan Mountain, Big Bald in the Bald Mountains, Black Balsam Knob (north of Milepost 427 on Blue Ridge Parkway), the grassy balds of Graveyard Fields and the Shining Rock Wilderness Area (which resulted from hot fires in 1925 and 1940 that occurred after the spruce and fir were logged from the area—MP 418-420, Blue Ridge Parkway), Hooper Bald on the Cherohala Skyway in Graham County (NC), and Gregory and Andrew Balds in the Smokies.

Round Bald in autumn 1980, looking north toward Jane Bald, Roan Mountain Massif.

Round Bald in summer 2012, same view.

The grassy bald on Tennent Mountain, Shining Rock Wilderness, resulted from hot fires in 1925 and 1940.

Grass and shrub "barrens" at Dolly Sods, West Virginia.

View from top of Big Bald (5516 ft.), October 1981.

HIGH ELEVATION BOGS, FENS, AND SEEPAGES

Large wetlands are rare in the high elevations of the southern Appalachians; large swamps are completely absent. Bogs are defined as acidic wetland environments, whereas fens are more basic in soil and water chemistry. Their floras, therefore, are significantly different. Seepages (where water seeps through a shallow soil layer), like bogs, are usually acidic.

Long Hope Bog, found in Ashe and Watauga Counties, NC, is perched in a high elevation hanging valley from 4200 to 4500 feet in elevation. It is a dominated by red spruce-Canada hemlock-northern hardwoods and harbors northern species such as bogbean (*Menyanthes trifoliata*) and cranberry (*Vaccinium macrocarpum*). Other bogs over 4000 feet in the southern Appalachians include Flat Laurel Gap Bog at 5400 feet west of Black Balsam in the Great Balsam Mountains. Here, a diverse heath-dominated flat (above Flat Laurel Falls) has glades dominated by sedges (*Carex bullata* and *Carex* spp.), bulrushes (*Scirpus* spp.), cinnamon fern [*Osmundastrum (Osmunda) cinnamomea*)], cotton grass (*Eriophorum virginianum*) and sticky asphodel [*Trianthera (Tofieldia) glutinosa*] with scattered red spruce. Boone Fork Bog near Blowing Rock is at around 5000 feet; and a red spruce bog in the Alarka Laurel area of the Cowee Mountains is just over 4000 feet. The Pink Beds at 3200 feet is among the most famous North Carolina mountain bogs. The site harbors one of the largest populations of swamp pink (*Helonias bullata*) in the southern Appalachians, a rich bog flora that includes marsh fern (*Thelypteris palustris*), the peripheral robin runaway [*Rubus dalibarda (Dalibarda repens)*], needlerushes (*Juncus effusus, Juncus gymnocarpus*), sedges (*Carex* spp.), and the rare bog rose (*Arethusa bulbosa*), an orchid. Seepages are more widespread than bogs in the high mountains and often have interesting floras. Kidney-leaved grass-of-parnassus (*Parnassia asarifolia*), round-leaved sundew (*Drosera rotundifolia*), and the deep-blue North Carolina endemic Balsam Mountain gentian (*Gentiana latidens*), are some of the noteworthy seepage species of high elevations. Although there are small fens known from the Mt. Hardy area in the Great Balsam Mountains, the only well-developed high elevation fen known in the region is the fen on Bluff Mountain in Ashe County, North Carolina. Here, at around 5000 feet, a spectacular wetland community of rare fen species has no equal in the high elevations of the southern Appalachians. Burnet (*Sanguisorba canadensis*), the rare large-leaved grass-of-parnassus (*Parnassia grandifolia*), spiked muhly (*Muhlenbergia glomerata)*, northern bog asphodel [*Triantha (Tofieldia) glutinosa*], and various rare species of *Carex* and *Rhynchospora* are present in this beautiful wetland.

The Cranberry Glades are an extensive complex of bogs in south-central West Virginia between 3000 and 4000 feet. Here, pitcher plants (*Sarracenia purpurea*), small cranberry (*Vaccinium oxycoccos*), cotton grass (*Eriophorum virginianum*), cinnamon ferns [*Osmundastrum (Osmunda) cinnamomea*], skunk cabbage (*Symplocarpus foetidus)*, sedges (*Carex* ssp.), rushes (*Juncus* spp.), and beakrushes (*Rhynchospora* ssp.) are present amongst red spruce, Canada hemlock (*Tsuga canadensis*), and white pine (*Pinus strobus*). Dolly Sods, also at over 3000 feet, in northern West Virginia has extensive cotton grass bogs with peripheral northern species of grasses and sedges.

Cinnamon ferns (*Osmundastrum cinnamomea*) in the Cranberry Glades, West Virginia.

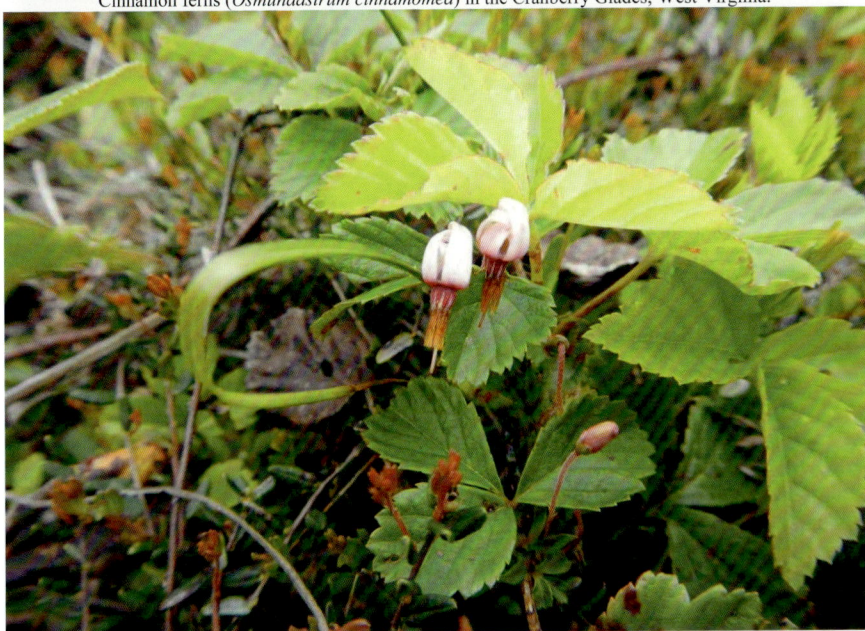

Small cranberry (*Vaccinium oxycoccos*) in flower, Cranberry Glades.

Red spruce-cotton grass-cranberry-cinnamon fern bog—Cranberry Glades (WV).

High elevation cotton grass-red spruce bog—Dolly Sods, WVA.

Fen on Bluff Mountain with burnet (*Sanguisorba canadensis*), grass-of-parnassus (*Parnassia grandifolia*), cowbane (*Oxypolis rigidior*), and numerous rare grasses and sedges.

Kidney-leaved grass-of-parnassus (*Parnassia asarifolia*) in a high elevation seepage bog.

Large-leaved grass-of-parnassus (*Parnassia grandifolia*) in a fen on Bluff Mt, Ashe Co., NC.

Appalachian mt. aster, Joe Pye weed, and kidney-leaved grass-of-parnassus in a seep in the Gt. Balsam Mts.

FLORA

ENDEMICS PLANTS
OF THE HIGH ELEVATIONS
OF THE SOUTHERN APPALACHIANS

Over 25 species of vascular plants endemic to the southern Appalachians are known from the high elevations of West Virginia, Virginia, Tennessee, North Carolina, and Georgia (see Table 3). Three high elevation species—mountain golden-heather (*Hudsonia montana*), Balsam Mountain gentian (*Gentiana latidens*), and Roan Mountain false goat's-beard *(Astilbe crenatiloba)*—are known only from North Carolina. Smoky Mountain manna grass (*Glyceria nubigena*), Blue Ridge goldenrod (*Solidago spitathamea*), Rugel's ragwort (*Rugelia nudicaulis*), mountain St. Johnswort (*Hypericum graveolens*), spreading avens (*Geum radiatum*), and bent avens (*Geum geniculatum*) are only found in North Carolina and Tennessee, and pinkshell azalea (*Rhododendron vaseyi*) is known from North Carolina and one population in Georgia. The ubiquitous Fraser fir (*Abies fraseri*) of mountaintops and the rare Gray's or Roan lily (*Lilium grayi*) of grassy balds are found only in North Carolina, Tennessee, and Virginia. Finally, the Biltmore sedge (*Carex biltmoreana*), granite dome bluet (*Houstonia longifolia var. glabra*), granite dome St. Johnswort (*Hypericum buckleyi*), and Blue Ridge ragwort (*Packera millefolia*) are known only from southern Appalachian granite domes.

The newly-described Balsam Mountain gentian (*Gentiana latidens*) is found only in North Carolina.

Table 3. Endemic and peripheral vascular plant species of the high elevations of the southern Appalachians included in the text.

SCIENTIFIC NAME*	COMMON NAME	HABITAT (at high elevations)	RANGE
Abies balsamea	balsam fir	mountaintops	NL to AB disjunct in VA
Abies fraseri	**Fraser fir**	**mountaintops above 5000 feet**	**VA, NC, TN**
Ageratina altissima var. roanensis	**Appalachian white snakeroot**	**openings at high elevations; high elevation coves**	**KY/VA to SC and GA**
Alnus viridis ssp. crispa	green alder	Roan Mt. Massif	Canada s to PA; NC and TN
Arethusa bulbosa	bog rose; dragon's mouth	bogs	NL w to SK s to SC
Aster acuminatus (see Oclemena acuminate)			
Astilbe crenatiloba	**Roan Mountain false goat's-beard**	**Known only from historic collections**	**NC**
Betula cordifolia	heart-leaved paper birch	rocky slopes and talus	NL and QC west to MN south to VA, NC, TN
Carex biltmoreana	**Biltmore sedge**	**granite domes to 6000 feet**	**NC, SC, GA**
Carex brunnescens var. sphaerostachya	brownish sedge	grassy balds, bogs, forests at high elevations	Circumboreal S to GA
Carex trisperma	three-seeded sedge	bogs and swamps at high elevations	NL to SK south to WV and NC
Chelone lyonii	**Appalachian turtlehead**	**spruce-fir and high elevation cove forests**	**WV, TN, NC, SC**
Claytonia caroliniana	Carolina spring beauty	moist high elevation coves and forests	NS west to MN, south to TN, NC, TN, GA; disjunct in AR
Diphylleia cymosa	**umbella-leaf**	**moderate to high elevation streambanks and seepages**	**VA, TN, NC, SC, GA**
Dryopteris campyloptera	mountain woodfern	spruce-fir and northern hardwoods	NL and QC s to TN, NC, AL
Epilobium ciliatum ssp. ciliatum	American willow-herb	bogs, seeps, disturbed wetlands	NL w to AK, s to NC/TN
Eurybia chlorolepis	**Appalachian mt. aster**	**spruce-fir and northern hardwood forests**	**WV?, VA s to GA**
Gentiana austromontana	**Blue Ridge gentian**	**high elevation forests and balds**	**WV, VA, TN, NC**
Gentiana latidens	**Balsam Mt. gentian**	**rocky seepages**	**NC endemic**
Gentiana linearis	narrow-leaved gentian	openings in spruce-fir forest and in high elevation bogs	Canada south to VA, TN
Geum geniculatum	**bent avens**	**seepages, grassy balds**	**TN and NC**
Geum radiatum	**spreading avens**	**high elevation rocky summits, cliffs, and ledges**	**TN and NC**
Glyceria nubigena	**Smoky Mt. manna grass**	**high elevation seepages**	**TN and NC**
Helonias bullata	swamp pink	bogs	NY s to SC
Houstonia longifolia var. glabra	**granite dome bluet**	**granite domes to 5000 feet**	**NC, GA, SC**
Hudsonia montana	**mountain golden-heather**	**cliff ledges at mid-elevations**	**NC endemic**
Huperzia appressa (=H. appalachia=Lycopodium selago)	Appalachian firmoss	rock outcrops at high elevations	QC and NL south to TN, NC, GA
Hypericum buckleyi	**granite dome St. John's-wort**	**seepage around granite domes**	**NC, SC, and GA**
Hypericum graveolens	**mountain St. John's-wort**	**grassy balds**	**TN and NC**
Hypericum mitchellianum	**Blue Ridge St. John's-wort**	**grassy balds**	**WV, VA, TN, NC**
Juncus trifidus	highland rush	rock crevices at high elevations	NL and QC south to VA and NC
Krigia montana	**mountain dandelion**	**cliffs and rock outcrops**	**TN, NC, SC, GA**
Lilium grayi	**Gray's lily, Roan lily**	**bogs, seepages, grassy balds**	**VA, TN, NC**
Maianthemum canadense	Canada mayflower	high elevation moist forests	NL to GA
Menziesia pilosa	minniebush	heath balds, bogs, rocky summits	PA south to GA
Menyanthes trifoliata	bogbean, buckbean	bogs over amphibolite	Circumboreal s to NC
Minuartia groenlandica (=Arenaria g.)	mountain sandwort, Greenland sandwort	high to low elevation rock outcrops	Greenland to NS to QC to VA, TN, NC

SCIENTIFIC NAME*	COMMON NAME	HABITAT (at high elevations)	RANGE
Oclemena acuminata (=Aster acuminatus)	whorled aster	spruce-fir and northern hardwoods	NL and QC s to GA
Oxalis montana (=O. acetocella)	American wood-sorrel	spruce-fir, northern hardwoods	QC to SK south to TN, NC. GA
Packera millefolia (=Senecio millefolium)	**Blue Ridge ragwort**	**granitic domes (usually lower than 4000 feet)**	**VA, NC, SC, GA**
Packera schweinitziana (=Senecio schweinitzii)	New England ragwort	grassy balds	NS and QC to TN and NC
Picea rubens	red spruce	spruce-fir, boulderfields, northern hardwood forest, bogs	NS and NB south to TN and NC
Pieris floribunda	**mountain Andromeda; evergreen mt. fetterbush**	**heath balds at high elevations**	**WV, VA, TN, NC, and GA**
Platanthera grandiflora	large purple-fringed orchid; plume-royal	bogs, seepages, and wet openings at high elevations	NL and ON south to GA
Potentilla tridentata (see Sibbaldiopsis t.)			
Rhodiola rosea (=Sedum rosea)	roseroot	high elevation rocky summits	Circumboreal to NC and TN
Rhododendron catawbiense	**Catawba rhododendron**	**rocky summits, shrub balds**	**VA and KY south to AL and GA**
Rhododendron vaseyi	**pinkshell azalea**	**high elevation rocky summits, cliffs, and heath balds**	**NC and GA (?)**
Ribes cynosbati	prickly gooseberry	boulderfields, grassy balds	NB south to TN, NC, GA, AL
Ribes glandulosum	mountain currant	boulderfields, seeps, spruce-fir	NL south to TN and NC
Ribes hirtellum	northern gooseberry	rocky forests	NL south to WV
Ribes rotundifolium	Appalachian gooseberry	boulderfields, balds, rocky forests	NY south to TN and NC
Rugelia nudicaulis (=Cacalia rugelia)	**Rugelia, Rugel's ragwort**	**openings in spruce-fir and northern hardwood forests**	**TN and NC (found only in the Smokies)**
Sambucus racmeosa var. rubens	red elderberry	spruce-fir, northern hardwoods, and boulderfields	NL west to BC, south to GA
Scirpus caespitosus (see Trichophorum c.)			
Senecio millefolium (see Packera m.)			
Senecio schweinitianus (see Packera s.)			
Sibbaldiopsis tridentata (=Potentilla t.)	moutain-cinquefoil, wine-leaved cinquefoil	balds, crevices of high elevation rocky outcrops	Greenland south to GA
Solidago spithamea	**Blue Ridge goldenrod**	**crevices in high elevation rocky summits**	**TN and NC**
Sorbus americana	mountain ash	high elevation forests, balds, and rock outcrops	NL west to MN, south to GA
Stachys clingmanii	Clingman's hedgenettle	high elevation openings	NC and TN
Streptopus lanceolatus var. lanceolatus	eastern rose mandarin, e. twisted stalk	high elevation cove forests	NL west to MI south to TN, NC, GA
Triantha (Tofieldia) glutinosa	northern bog asphodel	bogs and seepages, especially over mafic and calcareous rocks	NL s to GA
Trichophorum caespitosum ssp. caespitosum (=Scirpus caespitosus)	deergrass, deerhair bulrush	high elevation seepage (to below 4000 feet in sc)	Circumboreal; disjunct to TN, NC, SC, GA
Trisetum spicatum	alpine oat-grass	mountain cliffs	Circumboreal s to VA-NC
Vaccinium erythrocarpum	**mountain cranberry**	**balds, bogs, spruce-fir forests**	**WV to GA**
Vaccinium oxycoccos	small cranberry	bogs	Circumboreal s to GA
Veratrum parviflorum	**Indian poke, mountain bunchflower**	**high elevations woods and openings**	**KY, WV south to GA**
Viburnum lantanoides (=V. alnifolium)	hobblebush	spruce-fir, northern hardwoods	NB/ON s to GA

*Taxonomy from Weakley (2012).

Emboldened species endemic to southern Appalachians.
Abbreviations: AB-Alberta; NL-Newfoundland; QC-Quebec; ON-Ontario; NB-New Brunswick; NS-Nova Scotia; SK-Saskatchewan; BC-British Columbia; US states by postal abbreviations.

The southern Appalachian endemic milksick weed in the foreground, pale jewelweed in background.

Appalachian turtlehead, a southern Appalachian endemic, is common in openings on Clingman's Dome.

Umbella-leaf, another southern Appalachian endemic, is common in high elevation coves and seepages.

Appalachian mountain aster is found only in the high elevations of the southern Appalachians.

Blue Ridge gentian, here growing near the top of Mt. Rogers, the tallest peak in Virginia at 5728 ft.

Spreading avens (*Geum radiatum*) is found only on the highest peaks of North Carolina and Tennessee.

Bent avens (*Geum geniculatum*) is known only from Tennessee and North Carolina.

Mountain false-dandelion (*Krigia montana*) is found on high elevation seepage cliffs.

Granite dome bluets grow in shallow soil on granite domes in NC, SC, and GA.

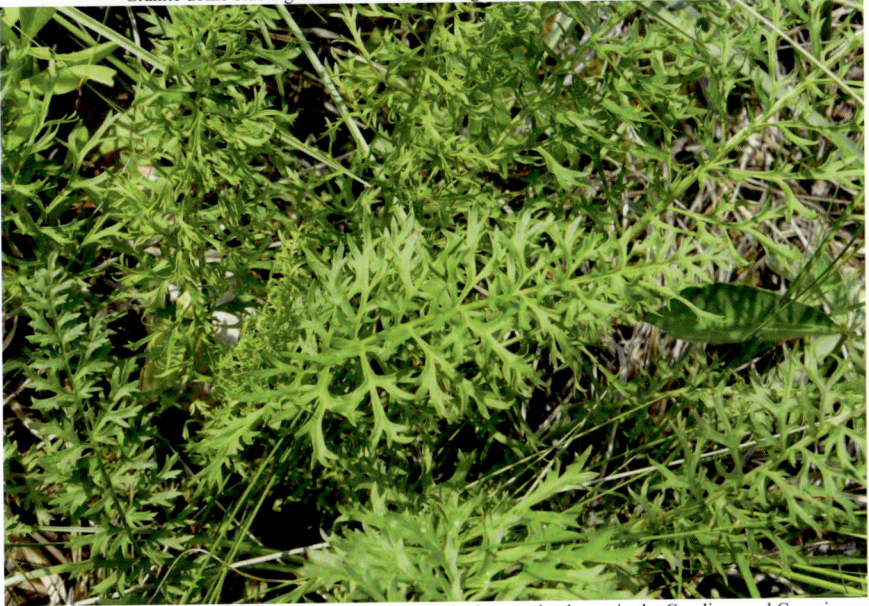

"Divided-leaf" ragwort (*Packera millefolia*) is also limited to granite domes in the Carolinas and Georgia.

Gray's or Roan lily (*Liliium grayi*) grows only at high elevations in NC, TN, and VA (image by Janie Marlow, www.namethatplant.net).

Minnie-bush (*Menziesia pilosa*), a high elevation southern Appalachian shrub.

Pink-shell azalea, an early-blooming NC-GA endemic, is common around Devil's Courthouse.

Mountain fetterbush, another early-bloomer, is also common on the southern Parkway.

Mountain cranberry (*Vaccinium erythrocarpon*) in spruce-fir at 6000 ft. on Mt. Mitchell.

Rugel's ragwort is known only from the high elevations of the Smokies.

The ubiquitous mountain buchflower, a plant whose leaves are more beautiful than its flowers.

Clingman's hedgenettle (*Stachys clingmanii*), a NC-TN endemic, on Clingman's Dome at 6600 ft.

Blue Ridge St. Johnswort is found on grassy balds and in seepages.

PERIPHERAL PLANTS
OF THE
HIGH ELEVATIONS OF
THE SOUTHERN APPALACHIANS

Many of the common species in Alpine South plant communities reach the southern limit of their ranges in the southern Appalachians (Table 3). Brownish sedge (*Carex brunnescens* var. *sphaerostachya*), roseroot [*Rhodiola (Sedum) rosea*], deerhair bulrush [*Trichophorum caespitosum* ssp. *caespitosum (Scirpus c.)*], alpine oat-grass (*Trisetum spicatum*), bogbean (*Menyanthes trifoliata*), and small cranberry (*Vaccinium oxycoccos*), all found in the high elevations of the southern Appalachians, are circumboreal species. They are found worldwide in high, northern latitudes, but also extend their ranges into the high Carolinas, Tennessee, Virginia, and, rarely, Georgia. Green alder (*Alnus viridis ssp. crispa*), three-seeded sedge (*Carex trisperma*), mountain paper birch (*Betula cordifolia*), Carolina spring beauty (*Claytonia caroliniana*), American willow-herb (*Epilobium ciliatum ssp. ciliatum*), narrow-leaved gentian (*Gentiana linearis*), Appalachian firmoss (*Huperzia appressa*), highland rush (*Juncus trifidus*), wood sorrel (*Oxalis montana*), New England ragwort (*Packera schweinitziana*), red spruce (*Picea rubens*), large purple-fringed orchid (*Platanthera grandiflora*), three species of *Ribes* (prickly gooseberry, mountain currant, and Appalachian gooseberry), red elderberry (*Sambucus racemosa var. pubens*), mountain ash (*Sorbus americana*), eastern rose mandarin (*Streptopus lanceolatus var. lanceolatus*), northern bog asphodel (*Triantha glutinosa*), and hobblebush (*Viburnum lantanoides*) are all high elevation southern Appalachian species that find their northern range limits in eastern Canada. Greenland sandwort (*Minuartia groenlandica*), of high elevation rock outcrops in Virginia, Tennessee, and North Carolina, and wine-leaved cinquefoil (*Sibbaldiopsis tridentata*), known from high elevation rock crevices south to Georgia, both range all the way north to Greenland.

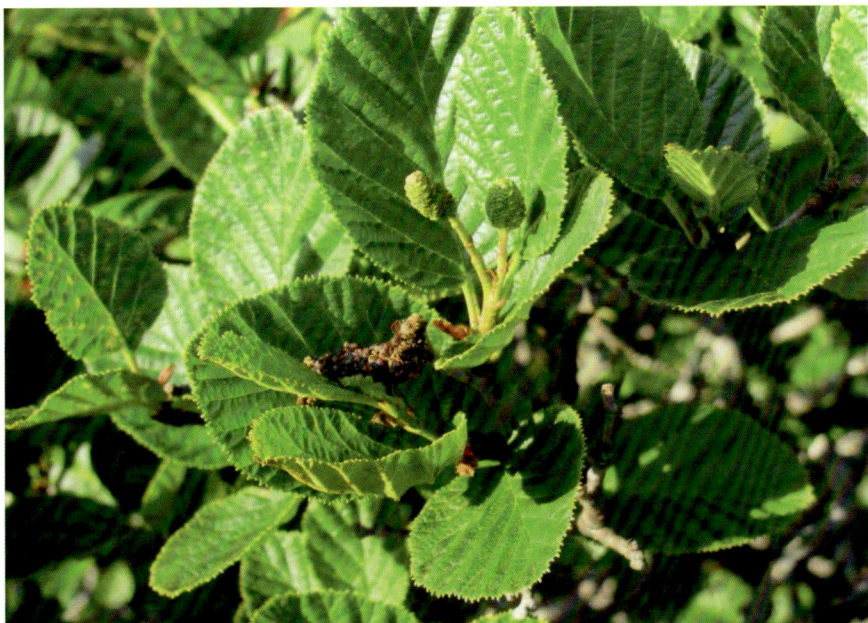
Green alder reaches the southern limits of its range on Round Bald.

Carolina spring beauty (*Claytonia caroliniana*) ranges from Nova Scotia to Georgia.

Mountain woodfern, common in the Spruce-Fir community, ranges from Quebec to Alabama.

Canada mayflower, common above 5000 feet in the southern mountains, ranges from Canada to Georgia.

American willow-herb, here on Mt. Rogers in VA, ranges across Canada south to NC and TN.

Cotton grass, a northern bog sedge, in the Cranberry Glades, WV.

Wood sorrel (*Oxalis montana*), a bright herb of dark spruce-fir forests (L L Gaddy III).

Whorled aster, common in Spruce-Fir and Northern Hardwood communities.

The cones of red spruce (*Picea rubens*), which ranges from Canada to NC and TN.

The liliaceous twisted stalk is found in High Elevation Cove Forests in the southern Appalachians.

The spectacular large-flowered purple fringed orchid is found in openings in spruce-fir forests.

Mountain ash (*Sorbus americana*), not really an ash, is striking in fruit in late summer and fall.

Wine-leaf cinquefoil, which ranges from Greenland to Georgia, grows in high elevation rocky crevices.

Deerhair bulrush is a circumboreal species disjunct in the high elevations of NC, TN, GA, and SC—here growing with granite dome St. Johnswort, a southern Appalachian endemic.

Hobblebush, a viburnum, is ubiquitous in high elevation southern Appalachian forests.

GALLERY

PLANT COMMUNITIES AND PLANTS
OF THE HIGH ELEVATIONS
OF THE SOUTHERN APPALACHIANS

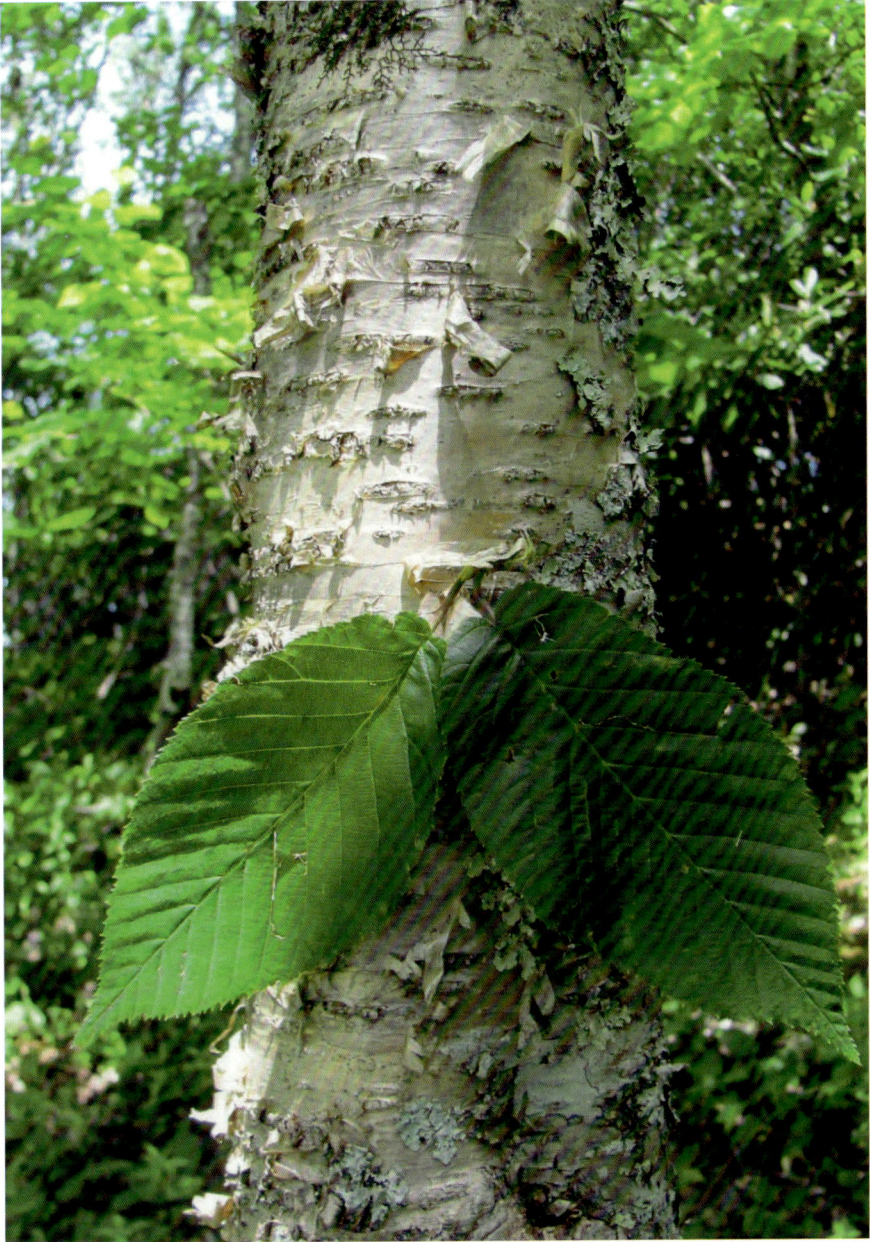

Yellow birch (*Betula alleghaniensis*) is found in most high elevation forest communities.

Bush honeysuckle (*Diervilla sessifolia*) is a common high elevation shrub.

Native sunflowers (*Helianthus* sp.) in late summer along the southern Blue Ridge Parkway.

Jewelweed, pale jewelweed, and lace-leaved coneflower (*Rudbeckia laciniata*) at 4500 feet.

Filmy angelica (*Angelica triquinata*) at 4500 feet in a spruce community in West Virginia.

Whorled loosestrife is common on Appalachian roadsides.

Turk's-cap lily (*Lilium superbum*) is often seen on seepage cliffs and moist roadsides at high elevations.

A large colony of trout lily at 5800 feet in Northern Hardwoods on the southern Blue Ridge Parkway.

Mayapple, dwarfed erect trillium, and Indian poke in Haywood Gap at just below 6000 feet.

White or basil bergamot (*Monarda clinopodia*) is common in the Smokies along roadsides.

Bee balm (*Monard didyma*), with its bright red flowers, often attracts hummingbirds.

Brilliant flame azalea (*Rhododendron calendulaceum*) on Round Bald, Roan Mountain Massif.

Great laurel (*Rhododendron maximum*), one of the most common shrubs in the southern Appalachians.

Northern wild raisin (*Viburnum cassinoides*) at 6000 feet.

Sand myrtle (*Kalmia buxifolia*) is a low-growing shrub that is often found on Heath Balds.

Painted trillium (*Trillium undulatum*) is common in high elevation acidic woods.

Large-flowered trillium (*Trillium grandiflorum*) is found in High Elevation Coves.

Erect trillium (*Trillium erectum*) with Canada violet (*Viola canadensis*) in a rich High Elevation Cove.

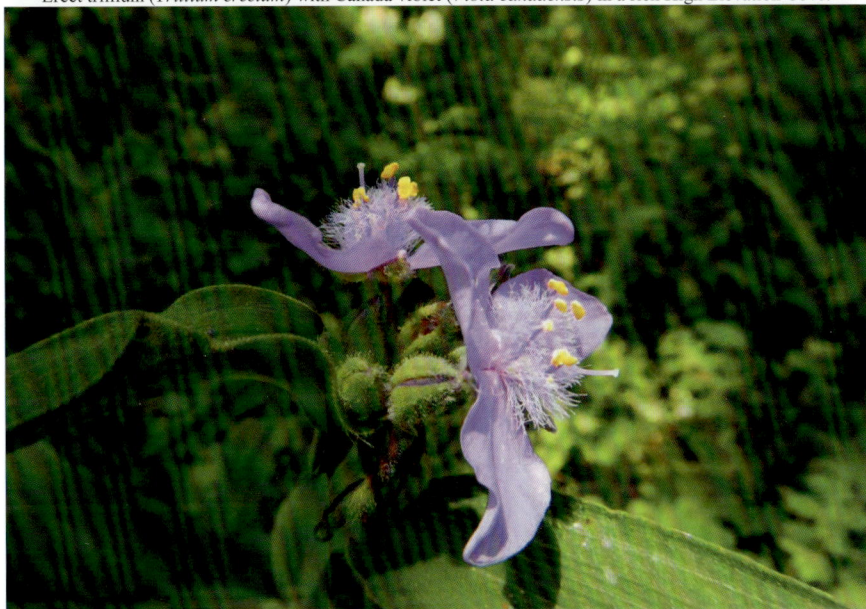

Virginia spiderwort (*Tradescantia virginiana*) is also found in High Elevation Cove Forests.

Low shrubs, trembling aspen (*Populus tremuloides*), and red spruce in boggy area, Dolly Sods, WV.

Wind and ice damaged Northern Hardwood Forest just south of Mt. Pisgah, Blue Ridge Parkway.

Gray dead Canada hemlocks framed by autumn colors at ca. 4500 feet, southern Blue Ridge Parkway.

Mountain ash in fruit, Shining Rock Wilderness.

The fen on top of Bluff Mountain, a one-of-kind place in the southern Appalachians.

View from Clingman's Dome: dead Fraser fir in foreground, dead Canada hemlock on the slopes.

Northern Hardwoods mixes with the Spruce-Fir Community at around 5800 feet—Mt. Hardy Gap, NC.

The Blowing Rock at Blowing Rock, NC, elevation 3840 feet, with scattered dwarfed Carolina hemlocks.

Sunset over the Great Smoky Mountains, view from Waterrock Knob, ca. 6000 feet.

Spring climbs uphill in the Craggies.

Late autumn sky, Big Bald, Bald Mountains, TN-NC border.

Dense autumn fog on Waterrock Knob in Spruce-Fir Community.

Mature, dwarfed pitch pine (*Pinus rigida*) on Big Fodderstack, a granite dome near Highlands, NC.

ACKNOWLEDGMENTS AND SOURCES

The plant community terminology used herein closely follows that of the *Classification of Natural Communities of North Carolina*, Fourth Approximation, by Michael Schafale (2012). A. S. Weakley's online *Flora of the mid-Atlantic and southern states*, www.herbarium.unc.edu/flora.htm (November 2012 version) was my floristic source. Dr. J. Dan Pittillo read over my text and made numerous contributions to this work. Mr. Tom Patrick contributed information on high elevation cove forests in Great Smoky Mountains National Park. Dr. Josh McDuffie compiled the excellent map on page 6. Finally, my son, L L Gaddy III, made several suggestions that enhanced the quality of this work.

Billings, W. D. and A. F. Mark. 1957. **Factors involved in the persistence of montane treeless balds.** Ecology 38:140-142.

Boner, R. R. 1979. **Effects of Fraser fir death on population dynamics in southern Appalachian boreal ecosystems.** M. S. Thesis. University of Tennessee. Knoxville.

Brown, D. M. 1941. **The vegetation of Roan Mountain: a phytosociological and successional study.** Ecological Monographs 11:61-97.

Busing, R. T. 1985. **Gap and stand dynamics of a southern Appalachian spruce-fir forest.** Ph. D. Dissertation. University of Tennessee. Knoxville.

Cain, S. A. 1930. **An ecological study of heath balds of the Great Smoky Mountains.** Butler University Botanical Studies 1:177-208

Cain, S. A. 1931. **Ecological studies of the Great Smoky Mountains of North Carolina and Tennessee.** Botanical Gazette 91:22-41.

Chafin, L. G. and S. B. Jones, Jr. 1989. **Community structure of two southern Appalachian boulderfields.** Castanea 54:230-237.

Clebsch, E. E. C. and R. T. Busing. 1989. **Secondary succession, gap dynamics, and community structure in a southern Appalachian cove forest.** Ecology 70:728-735.

Core,, E. L. 1949. **The original treeless areas in West Virginia.** Journal of the Elisha Mitchell Scientific Society 65:306-310.

Crandall, D. L. 1958. **Ground vegetation patterns of the spruce-fir areas of the Smoky Mountains.** Ecological Monographs 28:337-360.

Davis, J. H. 1930. **Vegetation of the Black Mountains of North Carolina: an ecological study.** Journal of the Elisha Mitchell Scientific Society 45:291-318.

DeLapp, J. A. 1978. **Gradient analysis and classification of the high elevation red oak community.** M. S. Thesis. North Carolina State University. Raleigh.

Dickson, G. J. 1980. **Composition and stand dynamics of an old-growth upper cove hardwoods forest in Walker Cove Research Natural Area, Pisgah National Forest.** M. S. Thesis. Duke University. Durham.

Fuller, F. D. 1977. **Why does spruce not invade high elevation beech forests of the Great Smoky Mountains.** M. S. Thesis. University of Tennessee. Knoxville.

Gersmehl, P. J. 1973. **Pseudo-timberline: the southern Appalachian grassy balds.** Arctic and Alpine Research 5:A137-A138.

Harmon, M. E., S. P. Bratton, and P. S. White. 1984. **Disturbance and vegetational response in relation to environmental gradients in the Great Smoky Mountains.** Vegetatio 55:129-139.

Humphries, G., H. E. Jolley, and J. Dan Pittillo. 1997. **Along the Blue Ridge Parkway.** Westcliffe, Englewood, CO. 80 p.

Horton, J. H. and L. G. Hotaling. 1981. **Floristics of selected heath communities along the southern section of the Blue Ridge Parkway.** National Park Service Research/Resources Management Report No. 45.

Humphrey, L. D. 1989. **Life history traits of Tsuga caroliniana Engelm. (Carolina hemlock) and its role in community dynamics.** Castanea 54:172-190.

Lacey, V. H. 1979. **A floristic study of Phoenix Mountain, Ashe County.** M. A. Thesis. Appalachian State University. Boone, NC.

Lindsay, M. M. and S. P. Bratton. 1976. **The vegetation of grassy balds and other disturbed areas in the Great Smoky Mountains National Park.** Bulletin of the Torrey Botanical Club 106:264-275.

Lynch, J. M. and H. E. Legrand, Jr. 1989. **Breeding season birds of Long Hope Valley, Watauga and Ashe Counties, N. C.** Chat, Spring Issue:29-35.

McLeod, D. E. 1988. **Vegetation patterns, floristics, and environmental relationships in the Black and Craggy Mountains of North Carolina.** Ph. D. Dissertation. University of North Carolina. Chapel Hill.

Mark, A. F. 1958. **The ecology of southern Appalachian grass balds.** Ecological Monographs 28:293-336.

Newell, C. L. and R. K. Peet. 1998. **Vegetation of Linville Gorge Wilderness, North Carolina.** Castanea 63:275-322.

Oosting, H. J. and W. D. Billings. 1939. **Edapho-vegetational relations in Ravenel's Woods, a virgin hemlock forest near Highlands, North Carolina.** American Midland Naturalist 22:330-350.

Pittillo, J. D. 1995. Pp. 137-152 IN Trettin, C. C. et al. Editors. Wetlands of the Interior Southeastern United States. **Vegetation of the three high elevation southern Appalachian bogs and implications of their vegetational history.** Springer-Verlag. New York, Berlin.

Pittillo, J. D. 1976. **Potential natural landmarks of the southern Blue Ridge portion of the Appalalachian Ranges Natural Region.** Western Carolina University. Cullowhee, NC. 372 p.

Pyle, C. and M. P. Schafale. 1988. **Land use history of three southern Appalachian spruce-fir study sites.** Journal of Forest History 32:4-21.

Radford, A. E., C. R. Bell, and H. E. Ahles. 1968. **Manual of the vascular flora of the Carolinas.** University of North Carolina. Chapel Hill.

Ramseur, G. S. 1960. **The vascular flora of the high mountain communities of the southern Appalachians.** Journal of the Elisha Mitchell Scientific Society 76:82-112.

Roe, C. E. 1987. **A Directory to North Carolina's Natura Areas.** North Carolina Natural Heritage Foundation. Raleigh. 92 p.

Russell, N. H. 1953. **The beech gaps of the Great Smoky Mountains.** Ecology 34:366-374.

Saunders, P. R., Editor. 1980. **Status and management of southern Appalachian mountain balds.** Proceedings of a Workshop sponsored by the Southern Appalachian Research/Resource Management Cooperative.

Schafale, M. P. 2012. **Classification of the Natural Communities of North Carolina.** Fourth Approximation. North Carolina Natural Heritage Program. Raleigh.

Schafale, M. P. and A. S. Weakley. 1990. **Classification of the Natural Communities of North Carolina.** Third Approximation. North Carolina Natural Heritage Program. Raleigh.

Shafer, D. S. 1986. **Flat Laurel Gap Bog, Pisgah Ridge, North Carolina: late Holocene development of a high-elevation heath bald.** Castanea 51:1-10.

Silver, T. 2003. **Mount Mitchell and the Black Mountains: an environmental history of the highest peaks in eastern America. University of North Carolina Press.** Chapel Hill.

Spira, T. P. 2012. **Wildflowers and plant communities of the southern Appalachian mountains and Piedmont: a naturalist's guide to the Carolinas, Virginia, Tennessee, and Georgia.** University of North Carolina Press. Chapel Hill.

Stamper, P. G. 1976. **Vegetation of Beech Mountain, North Carolina.** M. S. Thesis. University of Tennessee. Knoxville.

Tucker, G. A. 1967. **The vascular flora of Bluff Mountain.** M. S. Thesis. University of North Carolina. Chapel Hill.

Weakley, A. S. 2012. **The flora of the mid-Atlantic and southern states.** www.herbarium.unc.edu/flora.htm (November 2012 version).

Wells, B. W. 1937. **Southern Appalachian grass balds.** Journal of the Elisha Mitchell Scientific Society 53:1-26.

Whigham, D. F. 1969. **Vegetation patterns on the north slope of Bluff Mountain, Ashe County, North Carolina.** Journal of the Elisha Mitchell Scientific Society 85:1-15.

White, P. S., Editor. 1984. **The southern Appalachian spruce-fir ecosystem: its biology and threats.** National Park Service Research/Resources Management Report. SER-71.

Whittaker, R. H. 1956. **Vegetation of the Great Smoky Mountains.** Ecological Monographs 26:1-80.

Wiser. S. K. 1993. **Vegetation of high elevation rock outcrops of the southern Appalachians: compositions, environmental relationships, and biogeography of communities and rare species.** Ph. D. Dissertation. University of North Carolina. Chapel Hill.

Wichmann, B. I. 2009. **Vegetation of the geographically-isolated montane non-alluvial wetlands of the southern Blue Ridge.** M. S. Thesis. North Carolina State University. Raleigh.

Wofford, B. E. 1989. **Guide to the Vascular Plants of the Blue Ridge.** University of Georgia Press, Athens and London. 384 p.

INDEX: PLACES AND PEOPLE

(see Table 3 for scientific and common names of plants)

INDEX (cont.)